AS FAR AS I KNOW

AS FAR AS I KNOW

·
·
·
·
·

Joseph Somoza

11/28/15

Best wishes.

CINCO PUNTOS PRESS   EL PASO

ACKNOWLEDGMENTS

Adobe Walls, Assisi, The Blue Pen Literary Magazine, Chiron Review, Hamilton Stone Review, Harwood Art Center, The Honey Land Review, House Organ, Jenny Magazine, The Jet Fuel Review, Linden Avenue Literary Journal, Malpais Review, Message In A Bottle, The New Mirage Journal, On Barcelona, Redactions, Rough Road Review, Sage Trail, The Screech Owl, Sin Fronteras Journal, South Florida Arts Journal, Up The Staircase Quarterly.

COVER IMAGE: *Tao Chien Gazes South,* JB Bryan, oil on canvas. Collection of Dr. Janet Simon & Mark Weber.

BOOK DESIGN: JB Bryan / La Alameda Press

Set in Bembo.

FIRST EDITION
10 9 8 7 6 5 4 3 2 1

Library of Congress Cataloging-in-Publication Data

Somoza, Joseph.
  [Poems. Selections]
  As far as I know / by Joseph Somoza. — First edition.
      pages ; cm
  ISBN 978-1-941026-25-0 (pbk. : alk. paper)
  I. Title.
  PS3569.O6534A6 2015
  811'.54—dc23

                              2015024950

FOR
Ramona Somoza Suárez
(1916-2014)

CONTENTS

Say Something

April Flowers

From the Dark

Say Something

MAKESHIFT

How about if I just start?—
mosquito-spray perfume
    on my hands,
the dog next door
    making demands,
September partly cloudy
for some unseasonable
reason—
    although I'll take it, as
Studs Terkel would advise
when he was alive and on live
radio. But let's not dwell
sentimentally on the past or
passing, as my brain
likes to do when put on
"automatic."
My sinuses are stopped,
throat raw, mind somewhat
spacey, but I *do*
feel a breeze rubbing my face
and enjoy watching the swaying
rows of tiny locust leaves
draped over the cinderblocks
that cement my enclosure,
    my space and angle
on the world, the world I hear
driving by,
just past the house, quietly
now, but to pick up
at lunchtime.

As for me, there's nothing I
have to do, nowhere
to go. Right here
was always the best place
anyway
and I've arrived,
work-tools in hand,
or head: notebook
and pen, eyes, memory,
words.

LIVING THEATER

The sprinkler continues sending out its
arcs of gleaming water that
gravity converts to puddles.
It's like a story being told,
like the hero stories sung
continuously the thirty nights of Ramadan.
A fly lands on a sunny portion
of my notebook as I'm writing,
sitting in my yard in the denim shirt I wore
waiting on a bench for the museum
to open in Madrid after we had
tostadas with café con leche—

      years ago,
which translates to a million moments
such as this, each one a link to then,
and then.
      And then? The storyteller
pauses for effect,
unlike the way the story actually
unfolds,
each fold releasing all its secrets
naturally, necessarily,
without melodrama.

FLIGHT RISK

I'm not really "going away."
You're going *with* me.
One of those little birds with
a long beak just
flew by and
settled
on the pyracantha.
But now he's gone.
Now his name, even, is gone.
And now,
just like that,
"hummingbird."
Thank God
for words.
Even though they escape you,
they allow you to hold on:
"locust tree,"
"purple clamp binder,"
"flyswatter."
A red-throated finch
pops into the yucca and
sings
a multi-syllable song,
maybe from the Sudan,
or Iran.
I Ran All The Way Home.
Remember?
(on the car radio, while
"cruising"
Saturday nights).

Anywhere

Sunny, a few raindrops
drifting down
between leaves.
That bough across the way
would be low enough to
shelter me—
      if I'd been born a cat,
      although I'm not.
I'm an old man who, at this moment,
could be
      something else—
            that thrasher, maybe,
on the fence, who
flew away,
      but now is walking on
the neighbor's roof for his own
particular reason—that
      I would know, instinctively,
            if I were he,
and would look over at that
old man on a chair, suspiciously—
            who's me.

"I'm not a threat," I say,
but the thrasher has no use for
words. Can't build
a nest with them—
      like I can,
or a path
      to fly me places.

ACCUMULUS

It's overcast this morning,
a gray pall cast
over what should
be a new day's brightness.
Who says
it should be?
Who determines
what a day will bring?
A truck backing up
beeps its warning.
An old aluminum pan
leans against the cinderblocks.
If I wait a while, a word I'm
searching for might
float up to my consciousness.
You could call the mind
a pool. You could say
clouds are prospects.
The poem I might've written
might've branched off
somewhere else—
now a dead branch on a
language tree, or like my father's
aunt who never married.
We make too much
of things. We ourselves are
little things. Consider
the tiny ant you'll step on
walking back into the house.

Consider India, people
praying along the Ganges
for the souls floating upward
above bodies being burnt.
The Indian is an ancient culture.
It makes too much of us.
It's cluttered like my
mother-in-law's study when she died.
Think the barren Arizona desert
along your drive to California.
Think the impoverished
Tarahumara woman
begging on a stoop in Juarez.
Think of flowers that sprout
whether or not the rain
arrives on schedule.
The mind
will think its thoughts
regardless,
and the hand
will want to rain them down.

SPEAKING FOR MYSELF

It's all very interesting, what
"the culture" thinks,
through language I happen, also,
to be using.
        I happened also
and won't apologize.
My backyard made me
what I am today, or
enabled me, as much as
systems in my body
passed to me by
biological urges in my
predecessors
that I urge forward,
line to line, and
so forth.
        I cough.
Two white butterflies
liven the bed of flowers
beside the faded picket fence
where a pyracantha once
contributed to the "thicket"
that drew birds in winter
for the bright red berries
reminiscent of holly berries
in the Christmas carols
people sang,
        and maybe sing.
No longer in the loop, isolated

in my body in my back yard,
    I can't be sure,
I, speaking
in the language that
occurs to me, from whatever
sources.

SAY SOMETHING

What are you saying when you
say something? You're
saying something
and somebody else is listening,
maybe even just you, that part of you
that's all ears hears
something in what you said that,
earlier, was left unheard.
The said words live by
stimulating a mind,
maybe reminding it of what
it thought to say but, by not saying,
left the thought behind, un-mined,
in the dark of the mind, buried
in the ore, never to be
brought to light, polished, and spent
in conversation, passed
from mind to mind, the words
prompting other words to
come out
and be thought about,
passed on
from mind to mouth,
never to be completely spent.

NOW I SEE I'M REALLY

friends with all these people
I thought I knew only through
their books, their words
secreted by their bodies as
immediate as they lived,
impoverished otherwise except for
quick trips to the store, then
back to eat in the apartment,
the talk continuing with
this or that one also spending
a life on words, living
to write, though nothing that
intentional at first, just wanting to
live authentic, having been raised
in the culture's artificialness, even these
clever two-word phrases you can't
escape but try to
wrench the honesty from
what the moment brings
in the next line of random
sensation, which must be
the mind recording
life passing, channeling it
to the hand that works the pen you
learned to write right-handed with
although you're lefty. What better
to believe than what the pen
writes down, stabilizing
for the moment, the moment
passing.

FREE VERSE
—for Glen

I let the day go, it was so
beautiful.
I couldn't stand
tying it down with
lines that would
wrap it in place.
So I went out
shopping
and came back
to find the day
sailing with its
white streaks,
and its birds
doing what birds do,
wherever
they disappear to
to go do it.
The sheets had
dried on the line.
The chair in back
was waiting.
December's leaves
continued to
color the ground.
They don't seem to mind
not being raked
until spring,

and who am I
to try to convince them?
Who am I to disrupt things
as they are?

Suppleness

Digging for a phrase inside to
move me forward, a spark
to unfreeze my old-age
somnolence, more difficult
to arouse each morning, seemingly—
       and truly see
this autumn light reflected
on the surface of each
locust leaf,
and on the years of wear on that
wooden picket fence I've
sat across from, looking at,
since my neighbor built it
with his young son probably
thirty years ago.

These days I seem often
to be looking back, but the past
pulls harder the further
you move on. And
there's no cure. I can't
will myself in the direction
of my choice
as I believed I could
then,
       having the confidence
youth's suppleness instills,
the suppleness
       syntax can give language,

enabling it to stretch
around a corner and
divert, then run parallel,
in apposition to, without ever
losing sight of
its original desire.

KINGDOM, #4

I have to tell myself, *Not everyone*
sits outdoors in the cold in
winter and keeps his feet warm
with a woodfire in the chimenea.

I have to notice that I'm
looking up to where the locust
lets the blue sky through its
black, rococo branches.

By then, I'm into the saga of
the leaning tower of yucca, leaning
but still standing,
still providing a perch for the thrasher to
alight
near sunset, fold
his wings back, and
contemplate his existence,

or maybe mine,
or yours,
the sky's the limit,
but only seemingly.

And now a raven in the giant evergreen
caws hoarsely, maybe to
keep the story going, or more likely,
calling to his mate

to join the raven congress
on the lightpole above Montana Avenue
before this early Sunday morning
melts away.

The Private Lives of Words

I don't want to sound
"public."
I don't want, even, to pretend
to some importance.
So why set the words
down—preserving them.
For others?
Clarifying them
for myself?
Already, patterns
start to form.
The words, once
written down, call
to other words.
It's so lonely
on the long, blank page,
so isolated living inside
someone's head,
behind eyes that are
forever looking
at the surfaces of things
from their secure
outpost—wondering
how it would be
inside—
inside a locust tree, for instance,
or a hummingbird.
Even inside that old rocking chair
sitting in the living room
since it was bought from Mary,

the ex-neighbor, at a yard sale.
And it's stayed
against that wall, overshadowed
by the piano, hardly noticed
beside the shelves of multi-colored novels
that probably
commune with each other
nights—
Hemingway continuing his belligerence
with Fitzgerald. De Maupassant
chatting with Flaubert.
You get some words together, and you
never hear the end of it.

Time Travel

You keep doing, while time
    takes
        care of itself.

And while doing, you're actually
    passing
        with time

so that time
    seems to stand still—
    until you look up from your doing,
        and it's later:
            the thrasher is on the neighbor's roof now,
            a rose has opened,
            you've moved from point A to B.

Each morning, the morning passes
    this way,
    and you latch on to it
        as it goes—
            on its way to the past,
            to what is now
                done.

Re-minded

I'm reminded to write what
happens to me.
It happens to be
Bernadette
reminding me from her
book of sonnets written
       far and
           long ago.
Sounds like a song
blowing in, and because the wind is
calm I hear it
and because the sun is
tempered by leaves
I stay to listen
because the neighbor's dog stopped
barking to be petted,
being like the rest of us
       only more so, or what's this
sound my pen makes
if not
       loving barks?
I question mark.
I scribble sounds
my mind decides on, my mind
the judge
I trust.
Don't let me down, mind,
I hear my mind
tell me to say,
and I obey.

BACKYARD POETICS

A breeze blows and continues
to twirl the locust leaves.
The sh-shing sound that might be
wind through the leaves might also be
traffic. I'm in an urban back yard,
distracted now by the roar
of a power mower,
distracted but also engaged.
"This is what life is," seem to suggest
the medley of sounds and other
intrusions—a cat walking by,
a hummingbird suddenly,
a mosquito I'm forced to swat at.
The poem I'm trying to grab
hold of is emerging in this
place of distractions
where the black cat has just come
to lie down, as Jill
walks off with the empty
laundry basket, and the lawnmower
starts up again,
probably trying to finish
before the noonday sun makes it
too hot to mow.

ON YOUR WORD

Does it mean enough to you
(as you seem to think)?

Will you die willingly
(as you claim)?

Every moment that you
care to notice
the locust leaves glow

vibrantly in contrast
to the morning shadows,

as a dove hoots quietly
in the far away,

but not that far,
not so far you couldn't
walk there if you really
want to listen,

want,
and give yourself to

like you mean it.

STORY

The shadow of the windchimes
sways on the cinderblocks in an
      afternoonish kind of way, its melody,
dim and minor key, complements
the doves calling to each other,
         one tree to another, as the town
    winds down
another workday Monday, the sky
shining and unblemished.

    My role here, having just
returned to town, is not immediately
clear. Am I to be, simply, the
"recording secretary" as I was
in a high school sports club, keeping record
    of the days
    as they appear,
        or do I play
a more active role, act, so as to
move the story forward, the story
    of my life,
now retired,
often tired
    despite a Starbuck's coffee with Jill
late mornings and some
    early afternoons, the "story"
that no longer has a plot,
the lovers having met, the career
determined and run, the children
grown and on their own,

the conflicts all
            resolved so that the lovers
            are happily together now
                    forever, or until . . .
            see what I mean?
Is a surprise ending to this story
possible?
            Do I dare
come up with one and chance
            sounding gimmicky?
Or do I step
            off the stage, and continue out
the door, arm around my wife,
            and down the path of
day to day, each day
            as it comes?

SPRUCE

Embers remember
being wood for the fire.
No, they don't. *I*
remember
how the tree
smelled when I cut it,
the clean cut of the bow saw
across tree flesh
in the Lincoln pine woods,
Jill in her gloves
holding the tree straight as I
severed it
from its roots in the woods
to be carried away,
to be baubled and tinseled
as a life symbol—
and, later,
sawed into chunks
for the fire,
to be embered,
remembered.

April Flowers

THE FIRST MORNING

It's nighttime in New York.
They haven't known
each other long, returning home
from summer jobs.
They're without
reservations, and when the Greyhound
pulls into Port Authority,
they want off.

Something makes them haul
their bags and trudge down to the Village,
still too shy with each other to
admit to anything as definite
as a hotel room.

When they stop at a dim-lit
Italian place with checkerboard
tablecloths, they're
thinking they'll just
while the night away, then
get back on the first bus
in the morning.

But by 2 a.m., after a long day
of traveling, they're
exhausted.
They pass a run-down hotel and
he tells her he'll go

check the price,
        leaving her
        under the street light,
        holding the bag.
Self-conscious in the lobby,
he's thinking that the night clerk
notices
he's not wearing a ring.

2.

And then,
we're in bed together!
The novelty
makes us laugh!
You're wearing my
t-shirt as pajamas and we
hold each other, too tired to
consider anything
but sleep.

Later, a growling
wakes us, our arms still
wrapped around each other, and it's
morning
glowing in the window. We
scoot over on the bed to see
the newly sprinklered
street below, empty,

except for one pedestrian
walking with his dog.

Happily together,
we get up, dress, and
walk out to the city to
celebrate
our first morning as a couple.

EBB AND FLOW

The rushing sound of wind
disorients me and I'm—
          somewhere else, the Atlantic,
the night I left you and the kids
in the living room
and stomped down
to the shore, to escape the cozy
domesticity for romance, danger,
and destruction
those days I was at war.
The waves building in the dark
about to
crash on me, but I kept on,
terrified, my shoes squishing
in wet sand, as I dared
move even closer.

And then,
the bamboo windchimes
sound—
          and I've returned,
pacified, contrite, feeling
slightly foolish, longing
for the lamplight, your soft arms,
and the sweet
togetherness again.

Rear View

Now that the rain has all poured and
drizzled, making me feel I'm in
Chicago again, when we were first married,
still without kids, in our efficiency with a
Murphy bed that pulled down,
and the custodian, Mr. White, gave us
the three-legged soft chair we
fixed with a brick—

and we were fabulously young and
beautiful, and without a clue, except
knowing how lucky we were to have
found each other, though fighting and
making each other unhappy sometimes,
but that, too, adding to the passion and our
fierce alienation from the world
that we knew we'd have to
submit to one day—

uncompromising and willfully ignorant, we'd
go sit by the lake and let the glossy
humpbacks of water crash on the rocks, recede
and crash again until our shoulders and bodies
relaxed, and we could walk back
to the city, ready to accept whatever life
we knew was to come.

Us

When you're lying asleep
beside me, mostly
naked, as I am,
deep in sleep
(unlike me, who sleeps
lightly), and I
eavesdrop
on your living-in-your-sleep,
the part of your life I
can't share,
haven't shared our
fifty plus years together,
each night roughly for
eight hours,
adding up to
months, years.
And then myself am
pulled down by
the need to sleep
and can no longer
think or see
clearly but sink
into the pool of
quasi-thought and illusion that
translates, sometimes,
into dreams,
fragments of which
may linger
when, over breakfast,

we try to
share what is
un-shareable
of our lives

SATIE SETTEE

A pencil rolls
off the coffee table
onto the rug.
Except for the piano music
there's only
me
and a milky sky
outside.
A winter storm is
brewing and I'm
glad
inside this
house containing
favorite things,
my favorite other,
and space enough to
walk around.
Even in the dark
stumbling
we find our way,
or in the kitchen
by light of the refrigerator—
sustained
by a bowl of soup,
a favorite book.

ELECTION DAY
—à la Ted Berrigan

Take the glasses off, put them
down (I can read
      without them anyway),
see the world
      manifested
in a few backyard trees, faded
pickets, bits of houses, and a leaning,
      giant yucca (to add sex appeal)
this Election Day, such perfect
      weather I don't care
who wins ("we're all winning, we're
alive," said Frank O'Hara), Jill,
volunteering at Democratic
      Party Headquarters,
      calls people
to remind them to go vote, put
politicians in so they'll become
      incumbents
and be voted out, with
no big changes,
      though things
were fine to start—the cloudless sky, leaves
that turn,
      fall, and
decorate
      "the ground we walk on"—
to go inside, warm up
some coffee
      (with a cookie),
take a nap.

Out of Order

Because we weren't tired, I guess,
we got up, dressed,
and drove through the dark town
to have breakfast.
It was the time to be tired in this
middle-class town. The owners
of the cars that would've been
crowding the streets were still
sleeping. A homeless man rested his
head next to his coffee cup at IHOP
when we walked in. Even the one
waitress told us how tired she was,
working the graveyard shift.
The coffee she poured to "warm up"
our coffee wasn't
any warmer. You'd think you could get
coffee hot on a cold night, especially when
paying two dollars for it.
But the waitress knew the night
was for sleeping. Who were we
making demands, disturbing
the town's rest at 5 a.m.?

The Culture Wars
—after reading *Black Elk Speaks*

Just because you like the pretty green
doesn't make you
Indian—
or the glossy blue-black feathers of a
grackle perched atop a tree, who can
spring
without using his feet.
You think with hands and mouth
when making love, and can
tell time with your stomach,
but you're always
in your mind—even when you're longing
to belong to something
bigger, something other—
like the black cat to his
four-legged furry tribe. Maybe
somebody slipped up when they
grafted you to this
smooth-skin person.

FAITH

Those high scattered cirrus clouds
would never deign
to drop a few icy particles
in my direction,
would they—
down here among the boughs—
alongside the cats who can't
shed their fur
fast enough?
Even early waking in the dark is not
early enough.
Even the dark
is contaminated
after so many summer afternoons
built upon other
summer afternoons.
Where's the famous temperateness
of nature we learned about
in junior high school science class
that brings the changing seasons and the balance
of day and night?
The Pueblos even built their self-
contained system of philosophy and time
in observatories
watching the sun and stars.
They must've had an unimaginable
humility. That's
what would be needed to survive
summer
when your father looking down
is the Southwestern sky.

EQUIVALENCE

That little thought-current that
occurred to me,
or in me,
while walking from
shower to bedroom, that has now
disappeared—though maybe just
flowed downstream
and I can retrieve it
later. That's

how these Ravel piano pieces
strike me—like the trickle of
snow-melt
       down a hill,
trills lit by sunlight
flowing over obstacles, drawn
       invisibly.

Like the flow of
      this moment,
         to this.

MUSICAL BOATS

Only one red finch at the feeder now, and a gold
calls out from the locust, maybe
warning about the cats, who just
padded through the yard and out
to wherever
the day calls, clear and not
cold this winter morning,
the town quiet, just a hum that
occasionally—as now—clarifies
into a single car driving by.

My quarrel with friends I
differ with, even ones I love,
is ongoing. Must be what is meant by
"state of mind," the state
I live in, even in sleep—
and wake up from, hoping
to leave behind,
to have time for other
obsessions.
Yet, when teaching, I often
regretted having no time to
concentrate on my mind's workings—
"contemplation,"
a word with a more tolerant
suggestion: activity practiced
in the temple.

Words we use and where they
come from, not necessarily

where we are,
such as making do with a typewriter
in the computer age.
Improvise to survive. Adapt—
and so people
survive war, immigrate, and find themselves
in the American West, having dragged
possessions and attitudes along, to clash
with the attitudes of others.

Back in the "temple," a raven
caws in the large pine, as
he did yesterday,
though I don't remember
ravens living here any time before.
And now the finch is cheeping
in the locust again, and a freight train
howls from below—all of us
"in the same boat,"
        but on different decks,
                chugging along.

EVOLUTION

As I get older, the face
staring at me in the mirror
turns, more and more, into
my father's.
When he was alive,
I didn't know or care
for him much. He wasn't
interested in who I was,
or might become.
He went to work,
came home, shuffled
upstairs to his playroom
in the attic.
A pathologist, he taught me
respect for learning, and
irony. He liked
history, world travel, playing
chess, and young pretty
women he flirted with and
patronized.
I grew up as the protector
of my mother.
After I had children of my own,
my father died,
and my dislike for him
turned to pity.
Now that I'm turning
the age
my father never got to be,
his face watches me

from the mirror—I hope
in sympathy,
a trait seldom
revealed on that face
while he was living.

To Be Alive

"If I haven't been to Paris or Rome,"
is how I started yesterday. And I start
again today, this cold morning
in the back yard, the black cat lying
squarely in the sun.
In the biography I'm reading,
Allen Ginsberg is in Paris,
has been to Rome, and in the actual
world outside the book,
      is dead.
Has been dead for years.
A new crop of people have been born and
are growing in a world without
Allen Ginsberg.
He would never have believed it,
but, of course, to not
believe it he would have
      to be alive.
Or even to believe it,
or to change his mind.
      To be alive
is to be able to be
in Rome or Paris, and be reading
a biography of Allen Ginsberg
living at the "Beat Hotel"
in Paris.

BACK

In this image I have of my father,
he's pacing our second-story porch, smoking,
probably a Camel. Back & forth,
maybe thinking about his week at Bellevue,
where he's an intern again, an immigrant
forced to re-study his medicine
before they'll allow him to practice.
I watch him from friend Ricky's
porch across Clarkson Avenue.
I must be waiting
for Ricky to come out and play. It's probably
a Saturday, no school. Though it could be
the summer. Is it hot? My father is wearing his
usual white shirt with sleeves rolled halfway up,
hair prematurely gray. Later,
he'll turn practically bald.
He'll become a pathologist and
do scientific research.
In a few years, in college, I'll
switch from pre-med to English, not
wanting to be what he
wanted for me, insisting
on myself.
My father dead now twenty years,
I've become
whoever I'd be, and in a back yard
far away, I'm traveling
back through these words,
to consider.

Saturday Nights

Pretty black & white, hand-size, City Lights
paperbacks I love to
hold and look at!

I picked one up at COAS used bookstore
yesterday, Ginsberg's
"Kaddish and Other Poems, 1958-1960," and was

transported back fifty years, Chicago,
just a teen-ager walking with pal Tony
to the Uptown, hoping to pick up some girls
after the show, though how we'd
carry them if we actually "picked them up,"
having no car, wasn't clear.

Poor in means but footloose on the street with
hands in pockets, talking up our lives so they'd
resemble what we had
in mind, poets even then, though not
presumptuous enough to call ourselves that,

nor so self-aware as to realize
what we were saying as we talked while
walking to the corner grill on Lawrence for
fries and cokes where the girls were
everywhere in pairs or bunches.

     But we
not prepared to act definitively,

in no position
to make an offer, our shyness and
bewilderment over what must have seemed
an infinite potential resulting,
once again, in inertia.

STROLL

The sun is warm on the left
side of my face, so warm
I want to stay sitting
here in the chaise
in the far back
of the yard, away from
houses, street, a car
that might pass, or a neighbor
strolling—
if neighbors still
"stroll," as my parents,
in the 50's, took evening
strolls to their favorite bar
off the highway
near the Bayway traffic circle.
Funny, I should recall that
now, my father
dead 15 years,
my brother and I then
probably doing our
homework, listening
to evening radio, not having
formed, yet, concepts such as
"neighborhood bar,"
fully satisfied
at home, a rented 2nd story
place on Clarkson, center
of all things,
while U.S. highway 1, busiest

in the country, ran
all night
behind our bedroom windows.

April Flowers

There's such an abundance
of leaves now!
So many directions
a white butterfly
flits at the same time!
It's no wonder the cat
gives it up and
curls on a chair,
half asleep, half pretending
to sleep,
like old age in his
chaise longue, ruminating
while anticipating
lunch.
Where should we go
for adventure?
Is our everyday life
adventureable?
Must we travel far to get
somewhere?
What were the modes of
transportation we learned
in third grade between
reading comic books and repeating
a girl's name in our heads
walking home?
Home was
up the stairs, a small key
for the mailbox stuffed
with surprises.

Are there surprises left?
That tan-, rather than red-
breasted robin in the tree
seems so at ease
with all these
explosions!

Rain, After Four Months of Drought

It rattled the car roof and
windshield as we
splashed on the road to Mesilla.
It turned the world cold and
somber, and the trees, gazebo and
buildings on the plaza
into an Impressionist painting,
though with not one person
walking with umbrella.
We stood under the eaves of a café
smelling and hearing the world
transformed,
our senses of smell and hearing
transformed also,
the internal combustion engine
of our bodies, our closed
system of rivers and streams,
our private storehouses of memories
moistened
by the rain filtering
through the air, the less permeable
membrane of our skins,
and the various portals
through which the world normally
converses in a whisper
with our drowsy
interior regions.

WAVES

It's still summer. It's
summer once again. Summer
continues, though it
doesn't seem
as it was
when I was younger
and on vacation,
and even, sometimes,
at the beach,
where the girls were
in their bathing suits that,
since, have been discarded,
their bodies, even,
aged and been discarded,
though new waves
of girls keep
arriving at the shore,
new waves of boys that,
however, do not include
myself, whose boy memories
are the only
remnants of my boyness,
the only driftwood,
the boy discarded with his
lefty baseball mitt
and yellow football helmet.

In the back yard, new
finches keep appearing
at the feeder. Sunflowers

sprout and open up
their faces. The sky
renews its blue each morning
like the ocean
sending out another fleet of waves.

The Perfect Music

"Next I played it with the harmony of yin and yang, and
illuminated it by the light of the sun and moon. The
notes changed from short to long, from gentle to harsh."
—*Chuang Tzu*

My locust tree flies its plastic
banner of a Wal-Mart bag into
March like a lion

wearing grackles on his shoulders like
black epaulets on a motorcyclist
roaring out Picacho to the interstate.

The fire in the *chimenea* the color of
the red-throat finch atop the
leaning tower of yucca warms the

simulated leather moccasins I
wear to slip in and out of
scenarios, such as where I play

my father, a Spanish *señorito*,
cigarette in hand, overseeing
the painting of his

Chicago living room in the
apartment near the lake, where,
at dawn, I once dared

blow slow jazz across the water

so the sun could rise and uncloud
the mind of the sad girl

I had my eye on at school
but was too shy to crack
my voice for.

Luna the cat rolls herself in warming
sand far enough behind my
lawn chair to avoid what she most

craves, being touched,
as the sun's rising
makes the fence pickets glow

yellow against the grain stucco
of my neighbor's shed, the neighbor
who sold the place, hoping

to return to Greece, but since
Greece had changed more
drastically than he, he

was stuck
with what became of him,
what has grown on him like

bark, and made him
sad
and happy.

From the Dark

VEGETATION

That tall, listing yucca
may be looking at me—
        through the hollows in the dead fibers
that make up her scraggly face,
        beneath the green brush-cut
sprouting from her head with its
three antennae that flowered recently
        and dropped their seeds.

We've been facing each other
for many years of mornings now,
        to the tune of
dove monologues, and dialogues that
sound like monologues, and finch chatter
        whenever I remember
        to put the bird seed out,
across the patch of sand where
leaf shadows are animated
        by the breezes.

Today, Memorial Day, I'm writing this
        memorial to us before I leave.
Maybe when I return you'll have
        fallen over, smashed
on cinder blocks, and I'll have to
        chainsaw you to pieces,
drag you to the curb, and leave you
        for The Grappler.

Or, if I don't return, you'll continue
sending your cockeyed looks

toward the lawn chair by the bench
where I would sit, under mulberry boughs that,
from your perspective, might've
made my head seem to
sprout leaves. It's true

that I've begun vegetating.
The longer I've sat here
        the more I've grown resistant
            to moving,
the weaker the allure
        of distant cities.
If I could, I'd probably take root
        in this back yard
and let the seasons
        send their annual
            transformations over me.

Yearning

The sand between tufts of grass
could be a beach
if not for the cinderblock walls and
houses,
and streets that cross and
continue downtown
noisy with cars taking people
to offices without
windows
overlooking the ocean—
that is a long day's drive away.

The locust tree with boughs drooping
to the ground could be a bower
with trellised gazebo to
read in
while sipping iced tea and listening
to the rain
that hardly ever
falls here
in the desert.

The wind chimes tinkle
oriental melodies
faintly
whenever disturbances in the air
sail into the back yard
and through it
on their endless
circumnavigation.

ACROSS THE SKY

Now the little spit curl clouds I
showed Jill earlier have
loosened and turned
to fluff, with ghosts of blue
appearing.
A lone blackbird
flaps below the clouds, maybe
a cowbird, according to
the bird book, definitely not
a grackle, that I
thought made those
clipped-back whistles as they
fly in flocks, circling
at twilight—from one tree,
then settling on another—
the song cut back so
radically there's no
music left, just sharp, hollow
clicks across the sky
that set a tone of longing
as sharp as the flaming
pomegranate leaves,
the last to fall in the back yard this
day before Thanksgiving—
the floating clouds that may bring
rain tomorrow, when, after turkey,
we like to walk
along the riverbed,
that's mostly dry in winter.

SNAP

For a moment we stopped

after breakfast and just
looked out the back door.

Nothing happened.

No wind in the locust tree,
the cat lying on the welcome mat,
my tea cup empty after my
second cup of tea.

You didn't say anything,
my hand
resting on my cloth napkin.

It was as if someone
had come by with a camera and

snapped a moment of our life.

SPRING FEVER

The mockingbird's back,
and he colors the morning with
warnings and callings.
On the tip of the light pole, he
          keeps it up
while pollen-caterpillars
          drop
from the mulberry on to
where I sit, and where I don't,
          democratically,
and wind blows through the mint leaves
of the locust that are
          trying out their new
swivel technique,
dual-faced reflectors and
          conductors of
sunshine that must make the tree
feel good. They make *me*
happy just watching, fascinated
by how life knows
how to come back,
the way *we* know how to
          in the mornings,
having closed up our petals
at night, under covers where
smiling strangers can
          lurk
and dig the ground up
          from under,

leaving us
            high and dry,
so that we have to re-imagine
a trellis
            every morning
on which to climb down.

THE TREES

Sitting here among my friends
the trees, I feel their
quietude, the gratitude
they show by holding out
their limbs, generously
allowing the moss to grow
on them, and squirrels and birds to
build nests in their crowns.
They don't seem to mind my
sitting here, maybe sensing
how much I value their
contemplative nature,
their general satisfaction
with the way things are.
Rooted to their one place
in the woods, they don't
crave something better,
nor complain about the weather.
They stand tall and straight,
side by side accepting
whatever comes.

REALLY

Death really comes, facts
tell you, though
you don't believe it.
Robert Creeley really
died.
      Then,
Anselm Hollo.
There's a hollow
where they were,
         somewhere,
where now
         they're not,
(you tell yourself,
         still here,
the place
you always were,
         inside yourself,
for as long as you remember.)

Late Quartet

Beethoven must've been deaf
by then. But not blind—though
what does *that* mean?
That two negatives

don't make a positive?
Outside the window, sun and leaves
don't concern
themselves with my phrasing.

They're making love this morning,
turning sunlight to
maple trees
for later generations to sit under

the boughs, or look out
their windows
at them while smoking
pensively, as we did,

when cigarettes, cheap then,
made you feel cool, not
contaminated,
though everything you do

kills you
eventually. Is this why Beethoven sounds
so sad, so richly
melancholic, so continually

expressive
in the darker tones—that he saw
when he could no longer
hear?

DREAM WALK RETURN

In this recurring dream—dream
of a dream, or dreaming
that I dreamt—I'm
leaving here, you, this night, having
decided I will walk
to Chicago, across, first, empty fields but,
then, at cliff's edge overlooking
water, no place to
step but through a kitchen,
apologizing to the people whose
children show me their kittens, eyes
still not open; then, continue
through the living room and
out to where there's
space, a street, but then
remember that it's
night, moon glistening on dark water,
a canal I need to cross near
oil tanks, tiny lights on top and
refinery metallic superstructures
as in New Jersey childhood, try to
remember how I crossed it last time—
(was there a narrow bridge?) because past
the canal and beyond oil tanks are
city lights, Chicago, though where, what
street, which dim-lit building with steps
climbing to the door—knowing
I don't live here any more, yet
confident that walking long enough

along enough apartment buildings, alleys,
streets I'll find a door I'll know is
right to enter.

MIRAGE

Downhill toward the wharves
we discovered a whole new
neighborhood with diners and
old Highway 66 motel marquees
we thought we'd live in
for a while.

Maybe the neon and pastel
signs were of a vintage
corresponding with our urban
yearnings.
There'd be a chance to grow into other
selves with new morning rituals
along the avenues,
walking into antique gift shops, for
example, after having had our
morning coffee with a
donut, watching
passersby.

But our new personas wouldn't
manifest themselves.
Our cells and veins,
the cartilage
between our bones, couldn't
rouse themselves
sufficiently to convince us
that the sooty red
apartment buildings with planters

in the windows and iron
fire escapes were anything but a
memory from a previous life,
reverberating
in our eyes.

YET

Before the maple tree outside this window
rooted, or this building was built,
or the other buildings in this neighborhood
that now block the view of distant hills
against the sky—before Beethoven first
heard this "late quartet" I'm playing
in our room, hardly any part of this
existed, except for the waves
of the Pacific, then an unnamed ocean,
waves that had been rolling in
before anyone arrived
to build houses
with an ocean view,
on hills at the far end of a country
not yet a country, the hills
innocently leading down
to a beach no one,
yet,
had set foot on.

THERE

We went. We saw. We
had a lot of fun. We lived
a lot, or seemed to
fill the moments with more
awareness
of each moment
as it passed—on a city sidewalk
often—every moment wearing
nothing special or predictable,
no two the same
attitudes or steps, we noticed,
looking up.
The sky was there somewhere,
probably where it always was.
We didn't care
if she or I were the same
people we had known
before. So much
passing by
made us less aware
of self, more
conscious of each
moment going
so that another moment could
come up to us,
to be noticed.

Self-ache

What are those other
things running through my head
that shouldn't be there,
that I should disregard,
that probably make my stomach
ache? Or is that
biology, or aging, does everything
you live through make you
ache? Headache? Heartache?
Or is it the natural balancing-
with-pleasure act legislated
at your birth—since almost
anything the fingers touch they find
pleasurable, anywhere
the eyes look—
from this stone picked up
at the beach in Ventura to the more
complicated horsefly standing on
my writing book observing me
while I'm observing
it. Even that strand of grass
looks beautiful. But, still,
the rankling. Those used up
false heroic images of myself
I never managed to delete,
those social hungers of an immigrant
I shouldn't even mention they make it
seem as if I'm seeking
pity, which would be

pitiful, or, even worse,
practicing some stupid,
amateurish self-psychoanalysis—
though why should
self-concerns be so taboo?
Who can know better than I
how it feels "inside"?
Inside
but hard to pin down
where, except the all-consuming
stomach, or maybe the heart with its
allegorical history, the figurative ways
it's still used in the careless phrasing of
popular music—and I do belong among
the "popular," the people,
much as a distant signal
from the furthest back transmitter
in the brain keeps telling me I'm
from somewhere else, Mars
or maybe the moon, and somehow
stranded here among all these
others, whom I resemble only
superficially.

Thanks Giving

Those dark seedpods, wet from rain,
give the locust tree an eeriness—
the skinny, leafless branches also
dark wet,
the thick seedpods
pendulous against a sky infinitely
blue,
and the fiery
pomegranate leaves beside the fence
still intact on branches
despite heavy Thanksgiving rain
yesterday
and cleansing wind this morning,
another morning
to give thanks for
after the night's regeneration,
during which a dream figure whose
silhouette
I could see from bed had
walked up the back stairs of my
childhood
and was knocking—from which I
turned away, turning
on my side, and pushed against
the warmth
lying next to me in bed,
the smooth woman who shares days
and darkness with me.

DREAM

At 1725 Hamiel Drive
in Las Cruces, there's a door
with my name on it.
I turn the key in the dark, and,
when my eyes have adjusted,
see the spines of
paperbacks in a bookcase.
I walk up to
Esther Waters and fondle
her leaves smelling of mold
and old age, pass by
the couch and around the partition
to where the refrigerator
hums. It lights up
when I open it.
Hulking boughs quivering slightly
gleam through the glass panels
of the back door.
Whether any cats, or which
generation of them, will appear if I
unbolt the door to the yard,
I can't surmise,
any more than I know
how I got here,
from where,
why Jill isn't with me,
and who this person is that
still goes by my name.

EVIDENCE

A freight train's passing through.

I can hear its howling getting
        lower, weaker.

I think I hear the repeated clanking of its
        metal wheels on rail joints
        even from this far—

departure sounds of winter,

shadows of bare branches on the faded lawn,

a clay-colored chimenea with sooty mouth wide open,

leaves once living colors now drab brown
        curled in windblown bunches on the ground.

Why
        do I relish melancholy?

Why have I always done so, as I also relish
        walking in back alleys or along the rundown
        parts of town where one can witness
        people's makeshift efforts at
        brightening their dreary, boxy houses?

Why drawn to piles of discarded clothing, chipped
        dishes, and out-of-fashion books and lamps
        in the Goodwill store?

The part of a football game I like best
        is when it's over,
        when the stadium, half-deserted, is
        littered with refuse, evidence
        of a joy now past.

WOMEN'S EYES

What's the secret to unlock?
What you see
in women's eyes. May see. Some
women. Women's
are the eyes
you fish for, fish in.
As they do in yours?
Is the story simply
predator and prey?
Not simply? Neither nor?
From the beginning?—
that is only partly
knowable? Gnawable?
It gnaws at you and, thus,
the sound becomes a word,
a tool, a key.
But to unlock a secret
prior to words?
In the womb, the DNA-letters
are still to be
converted into
syllables,
pronouncements,
revelations.

SELF-SERMON

Remember
you're a person,
that she's a person too.

A person with personality,
stories that are personal,
"personal effects."

A person
has a private chamber
where only he or she
may enter,
personal tics and
moments when
she or he
is completely him
or herself.

Be grateful
when you're allowed to enter
another person.
Love someone
whom you allow
to enter you.

Whom, him, and her
are synonymous
    with holy,
the only old-time religion
worth living for.

GRAVITATIONAL PULL

Words that can be dense
as cinderblocks
or tentative as the swinging
bird feeder on which finches
twirl in my back yard
on an overcast day
the morning I sent a
change-of-address notice
to my mother's gas company,
which means she will be here
permanently now,
not leading her own life,
happily, somewhere far away—
or so I imagined,

so I could lead mine guilt-free
elsewhere,
not needing an anchor
so long as she had hers,
free to glide by the ocean
from where I could send her
cell calls,
putting the phone to the waves,
letting her hear seagulls
cry by.

Reductio Ad Absurdum

Anything the mind might
       grope for
under the sky of
       clouds breaking up
into a more-or-less
       checkerboard pattern
(like monkeys sitting at typewriters
       long enough
to re-write Shakespeare).

       "Long enough," of course,
being the problem.
       If Ma is dying,
           she won't be
eating any white or red grapes
for breakfast any more, or
listening to NPR (which I never
       convinced her
to do anyway).

       But her consciousness
of the world,
       the consciousness I
tried to gauge and
       free myself of since first
coming to know her,
       I won't have to
kick around any more.

HOSPICE

Ma continues dying
in her room. She continues
failing to eat, though never
growing any thinner.
Why won't someone
explain it to us? (unless maybe
they don't know.)

At the nurses' station, the nurses
keep busy with their paperwork.
The patients don't seem to
need them any more.

Every morning and evening we
come sit by her bedside and
wait expectantly,
any moment thinking she might
open her eyes and
speak, express
fear or resentment,
let us know she's hungry—
but she doesn't.

Her mouth opens wide as if to yawn,
but then re-closes.
Is it a trial run for
"giving up the ghost"?
Why would the body need to yawn anyway—
having so little to do any more
besides catching little breaths?

AFTER MA DIED

The sky is back, insistent
with its overcast,
but soothing
in its milkiness
under which doves
come and go like small
airplanes
looking for their ports.
At breakfast, I played
Mozart spinet pieces, purely
Mozart, sad
and happy.
In the dictionary, we
looked up "spinet," which,
surprisingly, has one *n* only.
Also, "clavichord,"
"harpsichord,"
"cembalo," pretty words
from places that the music
brings you like a
conversation
to make the room glow—
the kind of place,
I thought,
where Ma might be,
if she's still anyplace.

SPIRITS

If I start a conversation, maybe
someone will reply,
not the yellow
mulberry leaves the wind
blew down because
their time is over,
nor the sky that's always
mute though
striped with rib-like clouds
this morning.

A siren screams
rushing by,
setting off the backyard dogs.
It reminds me
where I am, my neighborhood of
stunted houses with
back yards walled in by
cinderblocks
where childhoods can emerge,
children grow,
and leave—
their home a place to
come to later
in their loneliness
and dreams.

Each moment as it passes
reverberates
like a ripple in a pond.

Trees keep a record
of their scars.
Even the dead
whisper in the dark.

As Far As I Know

Because she expected me
to notice details and not
be wasteful, I searched with my
fingers in the woodpile
and found these twigs and
bits of bark to feed the woodfire.

Having been warned to listen and
look around me when I'm out,
I hear a humming
engine and metallic scraping
that has to be
workmen on Montana Avenue.

After dreaming last night I'd
shirked my responsibilities
as a teacher, I got up early
and went to get the x-ray
I'd kept postponing,

as if someone
would be proud of me—I was
thinking when I wasn't thinking.

Or that she would love this
rustic view with chickens beside
the irrigation ditch, a scene
straight out of childhood
I walk alongside of
often.

DEATH DREAM

"Black milk at daybreak"
—*Paul Celan*

The pages I'd written were of
non-writing, volumes
of pages. And as I
walked through the dark woods I knew would
lead to the café where I could
read my non-words,
I saw that
death was the subject.

And I woke up
and went to the bookshelf,
and took down the deathbook
to serve as my guide.

FROM THE DARK

I searched along drafty stairways and inside
immense classrooms in the dilapidated
schoolroom building where visitors
experimented with paintings
of their own design—but nowhere
did I find you. And when, finally,
you appeared, and I asked you to sit
next to me on the stairs, your eyes
could hardly see me, looking so
fixed and
far away.

This morning, returning
to the waking world—you
in your studio after breakfast,
I, looking out the window
from the couch—it's overcast.
A chance of rain.
Spring winds rattle the junipers
and the old, toothless windchimes
hanging on the porch.
But there's a winter mood
in me—as if the dream
had taught a lesson I don't
want to learn:
"The people I most love
will die."

Winter Solstice

Is it still? Yes,
very still,
and the bush berries are
blood red
now that the blue
has blown in from the north
unobstructed by clouds, leaves, or
the heartbeats of sparrows.
The only escape
is the comforter, tousled and
soft on the bed,
like your wife's hair that
craves to enfold you,
as her smooth thighs would
gift-wrap you softly and
fly you
to heaven—where the heat
is turned up to around 75
and the cornbread and stew
are ready to eat on the stove.

WORK OF NATURE

The sun comes out from
under overcast. They say a cold front
will arrive—as if we deserved it,
as if we're given eyes to
see the locust leaves turn golden.
The red-haired girl the writer in
last night's movie
thought he had created
was actually a work of nature—
like our calico cat, or the way
thin clouds are brushed
across the deep blue canvas.

A girl like in the movie
did appear one day.
She looked and spoke.
So long ago you can't
imagine what you might've said.
She stayed and grew
wrinkled with you, two
backyard trees
beside a house, a nest
for children to
grow into their own adults.

That's how it was written.
We just follow what we know.

I'll Be Seeing You
—for Jill

Ten-thirty. The sky
a drizzly gray behind junipers outside
        the window I'm
looking through
        to two white columns
        that support the porch,
between which hangs an old
ristra
        slightly swaying in
currents from the rain,
        the rain that's
managed to cross hundreds
of arid miles to bring us this
        melancholy, intimacy
that, earlier, moved me to
put on the Ray Charles version
        of the song,
        on an old
record found at Walgreens
after David had been born,
        David, now married with
children of his own
in snow-buried Upper State New York.

Listening on the couch, we imagined
those two thousand miles—birds
        who leave their nests, years that
        pass and
accumulate, to turn the rock hard

stoics we thought we were
                soft and sentimental.
                                        "In
                that small café, the park
                across the way. . ."

The smooth backs of your thighs, last night,
as we sank spoon-like to sleep, I thought,
                are my keel—
what enables me to sail out
                to unknown adventure
                                and danger each night,
knowing,
as certain as it's possible,
I'll be able
                to return next morning—
                this morning,
with radio news in the kitchen,
the smell of toast,
a new day slowly
                lightening the trees.

So far.   For so long.   For as long as.

                                "I'll be
                looking at the mo-oo-on,
                but I'll be seeing
                                youuuu."

FREIGHT CAR

I'M SITTING IN THE LIVING ROOM WAITING FOR JILL to get ready so we can go get pizza, and I'm thinking of something to say about my poetics. What is something *about* something anyway? Something should *be* something is how I feel about writing. Wm. Carlos Williams said a poem is "a machine made of words." Prose "may carry a load of ill-defined matter"—like a freight car, for example—but poetry is "the machine which drives it." Who wants to write a freight car?

Similarly, Charles Olson said a poet's job is to take the energy of his/ her inspiration and convert it to poem without any diminishment of energy. "An energy construct," I think he called it. To accomplish that, one has to compose quickly. When I first read his essay "On Projective Verse," it was an inspiration. He articulated ideas I'd secretly thought about writing but figured I should keep to myself. Having been born in Spain of Spanish parents, and hearing only Spanish my first eight years, I lacked the confidence to consider myself a writer of English, particularly a writer of poetry in English. Yet here was a well-known, highly respected, experimental American poet spouting ideas about poetry that I fully agreed with.

That inspiration, as well as the example of poems I'd come to admire, made me re-think my method of writing. Rather than building a poem willfully line by line with the help of a thesaurus (as I had done my first years trying to write poems), I should allow the poem to build itself, allow words to call up other words through aural and memory associations and syntactic demands, and see where it would lead. I had known early that I wanted to become a writer, but not knowing any real writers, and having an exclusively scientific background, I had confidence only in a scientific approach to writing. Now, however, I began writing outdoors, in the mornings, to increase the stimuli to my senses and feelings. I brought with me books of poems that intrigued me, in the hopes that some bits of that language might prime the pump of my own language and get the poem going. (Frank O'Hara's irreverence toward the act of writing served as a useful role model in this.) And I began thinking of writing as a two-step process—the first step being free and unplanned, quick, intuitive, censoring nothing, allowing in whatever occurred. Then, as a second step, I would take the handwritten first draft indoors to my computer (earlier, my type-writer) and revise it. But this would be a careful revising after reading the original slowly, trying to understand what life, energy, and crazi-ness it had, so as to make sure not to destroy it. The revising would be to enhance the life of the original, highlight it through pruning, re-phrasing, re-aligning, etc. Following the examples of W.C. Williams, Robert Creeley, and others, I learned to use line-break to manipulate emphasis and nuance of meaning line by line. In this second phase of my writing process, I could utilize the analytical thinking I'd learned from studying science.

What I hoped to get from this two-step method—what I've liked about the poems that I like—is something uniquely poetic, in which the various facets of language contribute to an overall effect, to the creating of a language artifact the meaning of which can not be "translated" into anything else, an artifact that is what it is.

Being an immigrant who wanted to become full-fledged American, I also wanted a poem made from ordinary, spoken English, without excessively rhetorical devices, the kind of language spoken by my first heroes in America, my uncle Arthur and his buddies who would meet at his gas station in Elizabeth, New Jersey, regularly to shoot craps, drink Ballantine Ale, and recall their youthful adventures as merchant seamen—the "real language of men," as William Wordsworth called it. This would be a natural American-English language that an ordinary American in a heightened state of emotion might actually speak, a language heightened just enough to draw attention to itself but not so much that it would sound artificially "poetic," the kind of language a later hero of mine, Jack Kerouac, for whom English was also a second language, used in his novel *On The Road*.

It's been about 55 years since I first tried writing a poem seriously—a description of a prairie bird's attack on me in Wyoming, where my brother and I had found summer work at a lumber mill. I went for a walk outside town one afternoon and must've come too close to the bird's nest on the ground. I wanted to capture the incident and my fear. I was 20 and a pre-med major in college at the time. Later, when I read the poem, it felt good that I *had* managed to capture something of the experience.

Since then, I've written several thousand poems, developing an interest in the language itself as well as my own self-expression. Poetry led me to change my career plans from medicine to teaching English in college. And it led me to retire early from teaching (at age 54) in order to have more time and energy for my own writing. More importantly, the practice of writing regularly has helped me understand the kind of person I am and what is important in my life, what I continue to write about. It has helped me trust my intuition and feelings and provides a record of my experiences and changes. It has helped shape me. And, through this, I've come to appreciate literature and writers more fully, and, by extension, other arts and artists, and any other endeavor that helps make a person more human and self-aware.

.

Joseph Somoza was born in Asturias, Spain, and raised in
New Jersey and Chicago. He came to New Mexico State
University as an English instructor in 1973 and has been
in New Mexico ever since. Now retired from teaching,
he continues to live in Las Cruces with wife Jill, a painter.
Most mornings, he writes in his back yard while she
paints in her studio. Afterwards, they go to one
of their favorite cafes to compare notes.